25p

THE LIFE & TIMES OF RASPUTIN

THE LIFE & TIMES OF

Rasputin

BY

Penny Stempel

This edition first published by
Parragon Book Service Ltd in 1996

Parragon Book Service Ltd
Unit 13–17 Avonbridge Trading Estate
Atlantic Road, Avonmouth
Bristol BS11 9QD

Produced by Magpie Books,
an imprint of Robinson Publishing

Illustrations courtesy of: Hulton Deutsch;
Peter Newark's Pictures

ISBN 0 75251 567 5

A copy of the British Library Cataloguing in Publication
Data is available from the British Library.

Typeset by Whitelaw & Palmer Ltd, Glasgow
Printed in Singapore

There was little about the Russian monk Gregory Rasputin which was appealing. When he first appeared in the smart salons of St Petersburg in 1905, the 'miracle worker' from Siberia was a broad-shouldered peasant in his early thirties, with grime-encrusted nails, long unkempt hair and the coarse tongue of the farmyard. He never washed, neither himself nor his clothes. Unsurprisingly, he smelt.

Yet this same man was pursued by ardent

women, who queued to the bedroom of his apartment, the 'Holy of Holies'. Prime ministers gave him audiences. The Tsar and – especially – the Tsarina counted him an adviser, even a friend. And this influence with the royal family, the Romanovs, gave him unprecedented power; a power which would help to bring an empire to its grave.

It was something to do with his eyes. As everybody who met him agreed, Rasputin's eyes held a strange, disturbing compulsion. 'They were pale blue', recalled Maurice Paléologue, the French ambassador to St Petersburg, 'of exceptional brilliance, depth and attraction. His gaze was at once piercing and caressing, naive and cunning, far-off and intent.'

Rasputin was a natural hypnotist. For many, to look into his eyes was to be placed in his

Rasputin

mastery. Not everybody succumbed, but enough did. And hardly anyone, in the beginning at least, saw the evil which lurked in those brilliant eyes. Who, anyway, would have been looking for it? Gregory Rasputin was a *starets*, a Man of God, a poor wandering preacher. It was only when it was too late that the significance of his name became apparent. 'Rasputin' was a nickname given to him in the far-off village where he had been born – it means 'dissolute'.

THE HOLY DEVIL

Rasputin was born Gregory ('Grisha') Efimovich, the son of a carter. The year was 1872, the place the hamlet of Pokrovskoe in western Siberia, an unforgiving place of constant wind and climatic extremes, with winter temperatures regularly below minus 40°F. Although the peasants in Siberia, as elsewhere in the ramshackle Russian empire, had been emancipated in 1861, life in Pokrovskoe had not changed in hundreds of years. It was an elemental, eternal round of toil and poverty, where the only bodily relief was drink; for the mind there was religion. Even by the deeply religious standards of Old Russia, the Siberians were a peculiarly superstitious, spiritual people. Mystics and holy men were almost a local speciality.

There was nothing unusual about the early boyhood of Grisha Efimovich. He played with friends, he fished, he watched his father work in the stable. At the close of the working day, in the warmth of the stable, his father would often read out loud from the family Bible, words which came to enchant Grisha, and to lodge deep in his head.

When Grisha was 12, in bed delirious with a fever contracted trying to save his brother from drowning, he uttered his first 'prophecy'. A group of villagers, gathered around the stove in his parents' house, were discussing the theft of the sole horse of the poorest carter in the village. As the story has it, Grisha, deathly pale and his eyes glittering, suddenly rose from his sick bed and accused one of them of the crime. Rasputin's parents, Efim and Anna Egorovna, were apologetic and embarrassed, for Petr Androvich was an eminently respectable man. He denied the theft, Grisha was returned to bed, and everyone tried to make light of it. That same night, however, several doubting peasants followed Petr Androvich home and caught him hiding the horse in the forest.

Word of Grisha's 'miracle' soon spread. Whether his outburst had been occasioned by divine revelation, a sensitivity to Androvich's behaviour and words heightened by delirium, or observation of some earlier suspicious action, Grisha was accorded locally the status of a seer – a dizzying, unbalancing thing for a child.

As an adolescent, Grisha was more libertine than seer. He frequented the public house and ran after the village girls. His technique with the latter was unsophisticated: he would paw and propose sex. There were many refusals, but the sheer number of attempts brought numerous victories. At the age of 20 he married a fair-haired peasant girl called Praskovia Federovna Dubrovina, but his life continued to be as dissipated as before. Behind his back, the villagers spoke of him as 'Rasputin'.

Despite his dissolute night life, Rasputin was a diligent worker. He went into his father's trade, conveying passengers and goods over the long, straight Siberian roads, sometimes as far as the Urals. It was one of these trips which was to change the direction of his life. He was asked to drive a theological student, Mileti Zaborovski, to the monastery at Verkhoture. Impressed with the peasant's religious knowledge, Zaborovski persuaded him to remain at the monastery instead of going home.

As Rasputin quickly learned, Verkhoture was no ordinary monastery. While it was a retreat for monks of the Russian Orthodox Church, it was also a place where heretics were incarcerated and re-educated. Most of these heretics were members of the 'Khlysty' ('Flagellants'), a 200-year-old secret sect, two of whose beliefs were particularly troublesome for the Church: that those truly possessed by God were above the laws of Church and State; and that God was best communed with during the rapture of sexual orgasm. On Saturday nights, the male and female members of Khlysty donned white muslin shirts and retired into the forest or behind the thick curtains of an isolated house, where by candlelight they sang and danced, literally whipped, by the local sect leader, into a frenzy. At its culmination, these 'people of God' fell on each other in a wild orgy, regardless of relationship.

Throughout the years of his fame, Rasputin would be charged with membership of the Khlysty. He denied it, and it was never proved satisfactorily. But he was certainly influenced by them. Like the Khlysty, he would always hold that sin was the necessary precursor of holiness, for only those who had triumphed over the pride of virtuousness could achieve a state of grace.

After four months at Verkhoture Rasputin returned to Pokrovskoe, his head full of ideas. While he mulled these over, he took up farming as means of supporting his family (Praskovia bore him two sons, the first of whom died in infancy, and two daughters). According to Rasputin, one day while following the plough, he saw a vision of the Virgin Mary, surrounded by a thousand golden angels. Henceforth he believed that God had some special design for him.

His family were incredulous, especially when Rasputin declared that the vision had directed him to undertake a pilgrimage. 'Gregory has turned pilgrim out of laziness', joked his father. Nevertheless, Gregory walked two thousand miles to the monastery at Mount Athos in Greece, returning two years later, much changed. He seemed quieter, more

Mount Athos

reflective and was vastly learned in theology. Above all, there was an air of religious mystery about him. He had stopped his drinking and his public womanizing. In the dark cellar of the family farmhouse he prayed and wailed in lamentation. Neighbours called in and he blessed them; when they were sick, he knelt in supplication at their beds.

Soon the whole of Pokrovskoe began to believe that Rasputin had been transformed into a saint. The single exception was the village's Orthodox priest, Father Petr, who railed against Rasputin's heretical teaching of redemption through sin. Father Petr confronted Rasputin in his cellar and fled, convinced that the peasant preacher was possessed by the Anti-Christ. Now desperate, he sent to the Bishop of Tiumen for help. Soon an ecclesiastical commission appeared in

Pokrovskoe, with the Very Reverend Lord Bishop at its head. They interviewed the peasants who had attended Rasputin's cellar but met with a wall of silence. A policeman dispatched to bring Rasputin before the commission returned alone, converted by 'Father Gregory'. To the village priest's disappointment, the commission decided that, in the circumstances, it could do nothing and departed. But Rasputin was anyway tiring of Pokrovskoe, and left the village soon after to wander the roads of Russia as an itinerant preacher.

THE SAVIOUR

Rasputin first appeared in the Russian capital, St Petersburg, in December 1903. Rumour about his prophet-like gifts had already preceded him. He was a man, it was said, who having sinned and repented, had drawn extraordinary power from the experience, including the ability to heal. At the Religious Academy of St Petersburg, the Siberian *moujik* dazzled the seminarists with his pithy answers to religious problems. Rasputin was even received by Russia's most revered churchman, Father John of Kronstadt. A saintly man known for the power of his prayer, Father John had been the private confessor to the late Tsar Alexander III. An audience with him was a signal honour which many, in church, court and society, noted.

His reputation for holiness assured, Rasputin went wandering again. On his travels, however, he returned to his earlier habits: in Kazan, he emerged from a drinking den thrashing a prostitute; in Tobolsk he seduced the wife of an engineer. But such behaviour went unseen and unheard by St Petersburg society, and when he reappeared in the capital in 1905 he was greeted with rapture. The poor kissed his hands, touched his robe, crying: 'Our Christ, our Saviour, pray for us poor sinners!' And it was not just the lowly who bowed before him. The Archi-

Nevski Prospect, St Petersburg

mandrite Theophanes, Rector of the St Petersburg Theological College, impressed with Rasputin's gifts as a preacher, summoned him and introduced him to a very influential social circle around the Montenegrin sister princesses, the Grand Duchesses Militsa and Anastasia.

Russia at the beginning of the twentieth century was in a state of religious, superstitious fervour. Icons hung in almost every room of every house, and few people undertook even the most everyday actions without crossing themselves. This fervour – which explains much about the rise of Rasputin – was evident at all levels of society, from the bottom to the top. The Grand Duchesses Militsa and Anastasia, married to cousins of Tsar Nicholas II, practised a voguish form of mysticism which owed as much to the occult as it did to the Orthodox Church. Militsa, Anastasia and their high-placed friends yearned simultaneously for religious reassurance and a new excitement in their world-weary lives. Rasputin seemed to offer both. Their fascination with Rasputin only increased when he performed a miracle for them: he cured the Grand Duke Nicholas's dog of a mortal illness.

Soon afterwards Militsa brought Rasputin to the royal palace Tsarskoe Selo, outside St Petersburg. That evening, 1 November 1905, Tsar Nicholas II wrote in his diary: 'We have got to know a man of God, Gregory from Tobolsk Province.' Although impressed with Rasputin, the Tsar and Tsarina decided to consult Archimandrite Theophanes, who reassured them: 'Gregory Efimovich is a peasant, a man of the people. Your Majesties will do well

Tsarkoe Selo

to hear him, for it is the voice of the Russian soil which speaks through him . . . there dwells in him so deep a passion of repentance and so implicit a trust in divine pity that I would all but guarantee his eternal salvation . . . Manifestly God has called him to be one of his chosen.'

With such official blessing given him, Rasputin became an increasingly frequent visitor at Tsarskoe Selo. Used to the fawning of hangers-on, Nicholas and his wife Alexandra enjoyed Rasputin's earthy directness and bold familiarity. They were also anxious to learn what the peasantry thought and how they lived, for the future of the empire might depend on it. And the Romanovs badly needed advice. In February 1905, their autocratic regime had been rocked by strikes and unrest following the shooting of a priest and hundreds of workers

The Tsar

peacefully demonstrating for democracy. Nicholas had staved off disaster by introducing a limited parliament, the Duma, but there was still widespread disquiet at his rule.

Both Tsar and Tsarina came to speak freely with Rasputin – 'Our Friend'. To one of the officers of his guard, Nicholas explained: 'He is just a good, religious, simple-minded Russian. When in trouble or assailed by doubts, I like to have a talk with him, and invariably feel at peace with myself afterwards.'

The overriding reason, however, why Nicholas and Alexandra let Rasputin into their lives and home was their faith in his power to heal their haemophiliac son, Alexis.

The Tsar and Tsarina had already brought

one 'Holy Man' to the palace, a French ex-butcher's assistant called Philippe Vachot who claimed to be able to determine the sex of the Tsarina's unborn children. After four daughters were born but not the longed-for son, Alexandra was persuaded to give up his counsel. But before leaving, in 1902, Vachot told the Empress, 'You will someday have another friend like me who will speak to you of God.' In 1904 a boy was born, but a few weeks later their joy was overturned by their discovery that he suffered from haemophilia.

Rasputin was a far more impressive court mystic than his predecessor. Medicine had proved powerless to help young Alexis. But Rasputin could bring relief to the boy. In a typical incident in 1906, when Alexis was two, he fell in the royal park and bruised his

The Tsarina

leg. An internal haemorrhage occurred in his groin. For a week the child was near death, despite the ministrations of Russia's finest doctors. Then Rasputin visited the child and prayed beside him. As he left the sick room he said to the Tsarina, 'Believe in the power of my prayers, and your son will live.' Almost immediately the Tsarevich began to recover.

There were many other such incidents. Even those who distrusted Rasputin, like the Grand Duchess Olga Alexandrovna, were forced to admit that he could heal Alexis: 'There is no doubt about that. I saw those miraculous effects with my own eyes, and that more than once.' On one notable occasion in 1912 Rasputin managed to heal Alexis from afar. The royal family was in Poland when the boy hurt himself in a boat. Medical bulletins were issued to Russia warning that the life of the heir was in danger. Desperate, Alexandra telegraphed Rasputin and asked him to pray for the boy. A reply arrived the same day: 'God has seen your tears and heard your prayers. Grieve no more! Your son will live.' Again, Alexis came back from the jaws of death.

Perhaps it is not surprising that Alexandra came to view Rasputin as an emissary from God. Her prayers might go unanswered, but those of the *starets* did not. It seemed to the Tsarina that the life of the heir – and thus, perhaps, the dynasty – depended on Rasputin.

The mystery is how Rasputin 'healed' the Tsarevich. The most common explanation is that it was by some primitive form of hypnosis. Although it was already 1913

The Tsarevitch Alexis

when Rasputin took formal lessons in hypnotism, it was only to improve a skill he already knew he had and could use. Long before he reached St Petersburg, he had discovered that he could influence people by suggestion, his eyes holding their attention, his voice softly bidding them do his will. Rasputin would distract Alexis from his pain, soothing him with tales about Siberia, and then, tell him – gently, but leaving no room for doubt – that he *would* get better. Once the boy relaxed, the bleeding would reduce. Some, however, have suggested that Rasputin was merely a cheat who had an accomplice in the palace who signalled him when Alexis's sickness was passing its peak – for him to appear and take the credit for the recovery. As accomplice, the Tsarina's friend Anna Vyrubova, who also admired Rasputin, is most often cited. The drawback is that Vyrubova did not have the necessary medical knowledge.

The truth of Rasputin's healing powers may never be known for sure, but in the absence of better alternatives, hypnosis remains the most plausible explanation. It is interesting that Rasputin's daughter Maria, who lived with him in St Petersburg for some years, believed it to be the means by which he effected his miracles: 'The power, the nervous force that emanated from my father's eyes, from his exceptionally long and beautiful hands, from his whole being impregnated with willpower, from his mind concentrated on one desire . . . [were] transmitted to the child – a particularly nervous and impressionable subject – and . . . in some way . . . galvanized him. At first, through the stream of emotion, and later through the power of confidence, the child's nervous system reacted, the envelope of blood vessels contracted, the haemorrhage ceased.' This is supported by modern research on haemophilia which shows that de-stressing the patient causes the capillary blood flow to decline – in other words, the bleeding slows.

However Rasputin did it, the only judges who mattered were Nicholas and Alexandra. And they believed in him implicitly. His prayers alone could save their beloved son.

The seal of royal approval conferred on Rasputin secured his success in high society. Attired now in silk shirts and kid boots, with a gold cross hanging from his neck (a gift from the grateful Alexandra), Rasputin stormed the elegant salons of St Petersburg, fascinating in his coarseness. He liked to shock with exaggeratedly bad table manners. A secretary of Rasputin's, Simanovich, recalled the *starets* 'plunging his dirty hands into his favourite fish soup.' Such foulness only made Rasputin more attractive to some. As he soon understood, many society women found him a sensual change from their pomaded husbands. Conquest only begat conquest. Many boasted openly of having been 'honoured' by Rasputin. Every day, women trooped to Rasputin's apartment, where they waited in the hall for an audience with the 'Man of God'. A few were admitted to the admiring inner circle which gathered around the round table in the dining room.

The elect, numbering aristocratic ladies and close associates of the royal family, would sit enraptured, drinking madeira and listening to the pearls of wisdom which dropped from the thin lips of the 'little Father'. When he felt so moved, Rasputin would openly lead one of the coterie to his bedroom, the 'Holy of Holies'. Should the favoured one have any qualms, Rasputin eased their mind by telling her: 'Man must sin in order that he may have something to repent of . . . If God sends us a temptation, we must yield to it voluntarily and without resistance, so then we may afterwards do penance in utter contrition.' Thus he offered them the simultaneous chances to sin and be saved, allowing the satisfaction of their sexual desires, without the annoying doubts of conscience.

But such a religious confidence trick could not last for ever. By 1909 much of St Petersburg was up in arms at Rasputin's behaviour. His theological supporters were the first to withdraw. Archimandrite Theophanes, hearing the distraught confessions of women who had submitted to Rasputin, warned Alexandra against the Holy Man he had once recommended. Alexandra asked Rasputin about the charges. He declared himself innocent and acted hurt. Theophanes was transferred to the Crimea. 'I have shut his trap', boasted Rasputin in private.

The next theologian to withdraw was the charismatic monk Iliodor, who repudiated the *starets* after a series of unsavoury episodes. During a trip to Rasputin's home village, Rasputin bragged to Iliodor that he had kissed the Empress in her daughter's chambers. To support his claim, Rasputin showed Iliodor letters which he claimed the Tsarina had written him. The most incriminating of these – and the one which laid the basis for the accusation that Rasputin was Alexandra's lover – included such phrases as: 'How tiresome it is without you . . . I only wish one thing: to fall asleep, to fall asleep, forever on your shoulders and in your arms . . . I am tormenting myself for you . . . I am kissing your blessed hands. I love you for ever.' The letter was signed 'Mama' – Rasputin addressed the royal couple as 'Mama' and 'Papa'.

Iliodor was not to know that Alexandra wrote to all her friends in such gushing manner, and taking the letters at face value, was nauseated. For a while he contained his disgust, but when Rasputin raped a nun, Iliodor broke with the peasant prophet, and circulated mimeographed copies of the Tsarina's letters. Questions were raised in the Duma.

Like Theophanes before him, Iliodor found

that the result of crossing Rasputin was banishment. The *starets* complained to the Tsar and Tsarina of the injustice done him. Shortly afterwards an Imperial order bade Iliodor enter monastic seclusion. Also sent into retreat was Bishop Hermogen of Saratov, who had punched and beaten Rasputin with a heavy wooden crucifix as punishment for his violation of the nun.

Society, as well as the Church, began to withdraw its favours. The gilded doors began to close in Rasputin's face. One scandal in particular exercised the country. The *starets* was a frequent visitor to the Imperial nursery, ostensibly to pray with the young Tsarevich, and took to bathing the young boy's sisters, and hanging around in their bedroom. Concerned to see the Siberian peasant staring lasciviously at her charges, the under-

Rasputin

governess Mademoiselle Tutchev requested that he be barred. Alexandra's response was to dismiss Tutchev for questioning Rasputin's saintliness. But Tutchev spread her story, and the press began a campaign against Rasputin. Members of the royal family became deeply disturbed by the talk. Alexandra's sister tried to convince the Empress that Rasputin was a charlatan. But Alexandra would not believe any evil of him.

Nicholas was almost as blind to Rasputin's real nature. But he was also sensitive to the political necessities. At his insistence, the Imperial couple began a certain caution in their relationship with Father Gregory. Rasputin no longer visited the palace at Tsarskoe Selo – where he could not even be smuggled up a backstairs without it becoming the next day's news in the capital – but met with the Romanovs nearby, at Anna Vyrubova's house.

Such circumspection did little to dampen the uproar over Rasputin. The people wanted the Siberian satyr gone, the Tsar and Tsarina needed the Holy Man near to save their son. The gap between the nation and the Imperial couple grew, eventually to become a gulf.

THE POWER AND THE GLORY

Isolated from the nation, and even their own family, Nicholas and Alexandra came increasingly to rely on Rasputin. Not just in personal matters, but, little by little, in affairs of state and Church. This was entirely to Rasputin's satisfaction. At first he counselled passively, content to confirm Nicholas's own views. But then he began to meddle and direct. He persuaded Nicholas, in 1911, to elect the uneducated monk Varnavato to the See of

Tobolsk over the protests of the Synod. Emboldened, Rasputin nominated men for other posts. In time, all the main appointments in government and Church passed through his hands. His choices – based almost entirely on whether the encumbent was a crony or an opponent – were sometimes comical. A court chamberlain became Minister of the Interior because he had once impressed Rasputin by his drunken singing at a nightclub.

The Holy Man could break as well as make. Two prime ministers, Peter Stolypin and Vladimir Kokovtsov, were dismissed by the Emperor essentially because Rasputin did not like them. Such power made Rasputin a man to be courted. Once his personal protégé Boris Stumer became Prime Minister, the unofficial 'peasant Chancellor' virtually ran the country.

'Between these fingers,' Rasputin gloated, 'I hold the Russian Empire.'

Few disagreed. Anyone who wanted anything done in Russia asked Rasputin. His home was besieged by petitioners, from milkmaids to army commanders. If the petitioners found favour with the Holy Man, he would draw a cross on a piece of paper and scribble underneath it in his large untutored hand: 'My dear and valued friend. Do this for me. Gregory.' These notes secured jobs, releases from prison, and business contracts. As payment for help, Rasputin received whatever the petitioner could give, from the rich usually money. Over the years huge sums in roubles passed his way. Little of it stuck, and he cursed his hands as 'sieves'. For the less wealthy, there were other forms of payment. Wine and food were common-

Rasputin in St Petersburg society

place. Attractive women were expected to pay with their favours.

The petitioners were not the only people besieging the *starets'* apartment. On the orders of Prime Minister Stumer, the secret police set up a 24-hour watch on Rasputin. Ostensibly this was to guard his life. Yet even the fawning, doltish Stumer could see that some insurance against his master might be useful, and instructed the guard to gather all possible damning details on Rasputin. The squad of detectives obliged to microscopic degree. Their scribbled 'staircase notes' provide a vivid record of the *starets'* licentious life. Rasputin fornicated and caroused at a pace which would have killed a mere mortal.

Prostitutes were regular visitors. If the Holy Man's lust was not satisfied by a disciple, or a woman had turned down his advances, he sent out for company or roamed the apartment block like a wild beast. The detectives' notes were a model of deadpan sobriety: '2nd June. Rasputin sent the porter's wife to fetch the masseuse, Utilia, but she was not at home. Whereupon he betook himself to the seamstress Katia in Flat 31. He was apparently refused admittance, for he came down the stairs again, and asked the porter's wife to embrace him . . .'

Great bundles of such notes piled up on the desks of the police and ministries. They were eagerly passed around departments and to unauthorized people willing to pay for a peep at their salacious revelations. They were the talk of the town. As they gave exhaustive proof of his improprieties, they also seemed to offer ammunition for those wronged by

Rasputin, and those who wanted his downfall. But any such hopes foundered on the obstinacy of the Empress. She remained convinced of Rasputin's holiness. To her the 'staircase notes' were a fiction dreamt up by the commander of the police to blacken Rasputin's name.

Rasputin's position at court was not wholly invincible. More than once, Nicholas, under determined pressure from aides and the army, dismissed 'Our Friend'. On one occasion, when Rasputin had committed an outrage even he could not entirely explain away, he was sent on a penitential pilgrimage to the Holy Land.

The nadir in the *starets'* influence was the summer and autumn of 1914. There was an assassination attempt on his life in June, organized by the monk Iliodor, turned mad by hatred of Rasputin. Iliodor recruited a prostitute to do the deed. Walking up to Rasputin in the street, she plunged a knife into his stomach up to the hilt. With prodigious strength, Rasputin prevented himself from falling and fled to his house. A major operation was followed by weeks in which Rasputin tossed between life and death.

Thus the *starets* was away from court at the outbreak of the First World War, which Russia entered on the Allied side. Before August 1914 there had been a remarkable unity in the political thinking of the Tsar and Rasputin, and not simply because the devil-monk played the sycophant. Rasputin sincerely believed that an autocratic monarchy was the ideal form of government

The Tsar, Tsarina and Alexis

for Russia, since it was the one the vast toiling masses of the peasantry understood best. A democratic government was too complicated, too unstable for them. Nicholas was in perfect accord.

Where Tsar and *starets* differed was on the propriety of war. Rasputin was a pacifist. Not because of any high-flown beliefs but because of his background: as a peasant he knew that it was the peasantry who paid the cost of military adventures with their blood. Previously Rasputin had dissuaded the militaristic Tsar from embroiling Russia in war. In 1914 the tide in favour of patriotic military action was too strong, and Rasputin too weak; he found himself out in the cold.

He was soon back, his influence sweepingly restored by one of those pieces of mystical

Rasputin magic. One afternoon, the train carrying Anna Vyrubova from Tsarskoe Selo into St Petersburg was derailed. Vyrubova was found pinned under a steel girder, her spine badly injured. She was rushed to hospital, where a surgeon announced, 'Do not disturb her. She is dying.' Alexandra and Nicholas and her other friends waited by the bedside for her passing. Rasputin did not hear about Vyrubova's injuries until the following day. Then he rushed to the hospital by car, entering Vyrubova's room just as she was calling out in delirium, 'Father Gregory, pray for me'. Striding to the bed, Rasputin called, 'Annushka! Annushka! Annushka!' Slowly, she opened her eyes. 'Speak to me,' ordered Rasputin. She spoke a few, barely audible words. Turning to Nicholas and Alexandra, Rasputin informed them, 'She will recover, but she will remain a cripple.' Then, shaking and sweating, he left the room and collapsed.

Just as Rasputin predicted, Vyrubova lived but never walked without crutches. Her belief in Rasputin became absolute. The incident, too, only confirmed the Empress's conviction that Rasputin was a true saint. Ceaselessly, she tried to make Nicholas as convinced of this as she was. 'No, harken unto Our Friend,' she wrote to her husband in June 1915. 'Believe him. He has your interest and Russia's at heart. It is not for nothing God sent him to us, only we must pay more attention to what he says. His words are not lightly spoken and the importance of having not only his prayers but his advice is great . . .'

Many would come to blame the malign influence of Rasputin at court for the looming downfall of the Romanov regime.

Certainly, his policy of appointing placemen and friends to high office overburdened an already bureaucratic system. But his advice on the war was sound. He may have been a licentious charlatan, but he had a grasp of real life. The Romanovs, walled in their palaces, did not. Nor did the titled men who commanded the army. Rasputin warned the Tsar against the disastrous 1915 military offensive in Galicia, and when the peasantry of Russia had bled too much, he cautioned Nicholas, 'It is getting empty in the villages.'

As the war wore on, Rasputin recognized that the people wanted peace and bread. Hunger in the cities, he saw, was a problem of distribution. He persuaded the Tsar, through Alexandra, to cancel all passenger trains for three days in October 1915 to let supplies of food and fuel into the major cities. This piece

A room in Tsarkoe Selo

of ruling sanity was followed by few others. Nicholas neither cared about nor concerned himself with the lives of the people. Others did. Among those sensing the bitter, weary mood of the nation were the Marxist revolutionaries of Lenin's Bolshevik Party.

And ultimately, Rasputin cared more for his own indulgence and career than the fate of the people from whom he had sprung. Most of Rasputin's effort at court in the years 1915–16 was spent on insinuating himself into the good graces of the Imperial couple, especially Alexandra. He took infinite care to show only a face of piety at Tsarskoe Selo. However drunk or debauched he was , when a telephone call came from the palace, he sobered up immediately and rushed to the Empress's side. The act of piety was improved by a constant stream of reassuring words, which ingenuously melded prophecy and wisdom: '. . . Do not fear our present embarrassments, the protection of the Holy Mother is over you . . . Be crowned with earthly happiness, the heavenly wreaths will follow.'

Piety and warm words did not exhaust Rasputin's repertoire of devices to ensure his position. He was quite capable of veiled threats. 'Remember,' he once told the Empress, 'that I need neither the Emperor nor yourself. If you abandon me to my enemies, it will not worry me. I am quite able to cope with them. But neither the Emperor nor you can do without me. If I am not there to protect you, you will lose your son and your crown within six months.'

Rasputin's performance was faultless, and the Tsarina was completely duped. Although, in time, every piece of tittle-tattle concerning Rasputin was brought to her ears, she refused to believe any of it. How could she? The man was a saint who had saved her son and her friend.

THE REVOLT

By the autumn of 1916, the Russian army had all but lost its capacity to fight. Casualties ran into millions. Every day thousands of demoralized, ill-led soldiers surrendered to the Germans and Austro-Hungarians.

Collapse at the front was matched by chaos at the rear. Ministers came and went in droves. The railway system barely worked. Inflation and food shortages were a growing burden for the majority, particularly the workers clustered

Trotsky

in St Petersburg and Moscow. A wave of strikes had broken out. Ominously, the cry 'Down with the Tsar' was beginning to be heard once more in Russia.

But not everyone was suffering. As Leon Trotsky, soon with Lenin to lead the Bolshevik overthrow of the regime, noted with characteristic vigour: 'Enormous fortunes arose out of the bloody foam . . . in no other season were such gowns to be seen as in the winter of 1915–16, and never were so many diamonds purchased . . . everybody splashed about in the bloody mud . . .'

Splashing about more than most was Gregory Rasputin, the most odious figure in an odious regime. The so-called monk's excesses had hardly been touched by the war. To the poor, the moral corruption of the Romanovs was

Lenin

confirmed by the friendship they offered the 'Holy Devil'. But they weren't alone in loathing Rasputin. He had managed to make enemies of everyone, save for his own disciples and the Romanovs. The Church hated him for his insults; the army disliked his interfering, which included the sacking of the Grand Duke Nicholas as Commander, a man who had dared turn against Rasputin and suggested 'he should be hung'; the aristocracy despised him because of his familiarity with 'Mama and Papa', and because he dared suggest that they should fight in the trenches rather than walk round in the safety of the capital; and democrats hated him because he blocked the recall of parliament. Moreover, someone had to be blamed for the mess that was Russia's war. A scapegoat was needed. Rasputin was it. In the minds of many, the conviction grew that Rasputin must be removed. As the *starets*, blithely unaware, danced, drank and listened to his beloved gypsy choirs, intrigues tightened around him. There were two principal plots to murder Rasputin in late 1916, one official – or at least inspired by members of the government – and the other an aristocratic conspiracy led by a bored, immature nobleman.

The official assassination attempt centred on Khvostov, the fat chamberlain whose bass voice Rasputin had liked so much that he had him made Minister of the Interior. Unknown to Rasputin, Khvostov was intensely ambitious and had decided that he should be Prime Minister. To this end Khvostov did everything possible to have the Duma convened. His reasoning was brilliantly simple. The incumbent Prime Minister, old Goremykin, disliked intensely the rough-

and-tumble of parliamentary debate. The Duma, given the state of the nation, was bound to be stormy. It followed that Goremykin would be shown to be incompetent and retire – and Khvostov would step into the job.

The problem lay in convincing Rasputin that the Duma should be reopened. Khvostov dined with Rasputin several times, and several times seemingly won him over, only to find that Rasputin had not changed his mind. Khvostov became increasingly frustrated. To attain his objective, he tried to have the *starets* leave the capital, thinking he would carry out the plan in his absence. Over another fish supper, Khvostov suggested to Rasputin that he undertake a tour of monasteries as a means of re-establishing his religious prestige – he would pay Rasputin's travelling expenses, as the tour was official business. Rasputin nodded his agreement. The next morning, Rasputin was given 5000 roubles for his religious journey. Days, and then weeks passed, but still Rasputin did not go. Impatient, Khvostov asked him when he might be setting out. The *starets* replied amiably that he had no intention of going away. Khvostov decided Rasputin must be murdered.

As the Minister of the Interior and head of the secret police, Khvostov was ideally placed to arrange the demise of the monk. His plan was to lure Rasputin into a secret-service car posing as a taxi and drive with him to the country, where two masked men would be waiting. They would chloroform Rasputin and then strangle him with a rope. Khvostov issued orders to his staff to carry out the murder on this basis. Preparations began immediately.

For a short while the secret service flirted with Khvostov's risible plan but then got cold feet. It lacked sophistication, it was impracticable and it left too many leads. Fearing that it had compromised itself, the secret service then betrayed Khovstov to Rasputin and the Emperor. The latter dismissed the Minister of the Interior with the message that he was lucky to have his life.

When Rasputin was told of the Khvostov affair he laughed out loud. So mistrustful had his enemies become that they had frustrated their own plot to kill him, without the *starets* having to lift a hand. Quite possibly he was still chuckling when he took tea, as was his regular custom, with Munia Golovina and her mother in their drawing-room on the Winter Canal. Munia and her mother were among Rasputin's most admiring disciples, certain that he was the reincarnation of the Lord himself. The other regular guest there, Prince Yusopov, was emphatically not an admirer.

There was something boyish about Prince Felix Felixovich Yusupov, although he was touching his late twenties. Pale-skinned, clean-shaven, he looked for the world like a dreamy, bookish student. In fact, he was one of the richest men in the kingdom, thanks to his marriage to Irina Alexandrovna, the Tsar's niece. He was devoted to his wife. But he was also devoted to Munia Golovina, who was to have married his dead brother. The way the unwashed *moujik* manhandled Munia revolted him. So did his familiar talk about 'Mama and

Papa' and his contemptuous opinions on aristocrats and generals.

For the sake of Munia, Yusupov met Rasputin many times in her drawing-room, but his loathing of the monk only intensified. The only answer seemed to be to murder Rasputin. Not just for the sake of Munia but, as he told himself, for the sake of Russia. There was another, less idealistic reason for such an act. Yusupov was bored with a life of luxury that seemed to have little consequence. To kill Rasputin would be a great excitement.

Rasputin at the centre of a tea party

THE MURDER

The idea of killing him took possession of Yusupov. Helpers for the patriotic deed were easy to find. Grand Duke Dimitri Pavlovich, a member of the Imperial family and a very close friend, was admitted to the plot at once. Towards the end of 1916, Yusupov read of a particularly violent attack on Rasputin uttered by a monarchist Duma deputy, Purishkevich, whose hopes for ministerial post had been disappointed by Rasputin. Yusupov visited Purishkevich at his office at the Russian Red Cross and asked him to join the plot. Purishkevich agreed enthusiastically, and recommended that his assistant, the physician Dr Lazovert, also be invited. Sukhotin, a cavalry officer, and Nefedov, Yusupov's valet, were also recruited.

There was little danger to Purishkevich, Lazovert, Sukhotin and Nefedov in joining the plot. Because Grand Duke Dimitri Pavlovich was a blood member of the Imperial family, he was not subject to ordinary law, and this immunity extended to all other participators in a criminal act in which the Romanov was involved.

The innocent pawns in Yusupov's plan were the Golovins. Through them the prince could get close to Rasputin and win his trust. Yusupov visited the Golovins, and lightly dropped a hint that he would not mind meeting the *starets* again. Delighted that the Prince seemed to be warming to Rasputin, the Golovins arranged a tea for both men the next day. Felix feigned friendliness, while Rasputin was charmed to find that the young Prince played the guitar, and listened happily to his playing. The two men left the house agreeing to meet again soon.

Yusupov and his conspirators began to put the rest of the plot into motion. Poison, easily obtained without suspicion by Dr Lazoverts, seemed the appropriate method. The ideal scene for the crime was judged to be Yusupov's own palace on the Moika, where the cellar vaults were undergoing alterations. One room was furnished as a dining-room and made to look as though it was always lived in. Once Rasputin was lured there, Yusupov would feed him poison. When he was dead, the others – waiting upstairs – would come down and wrap his body in chains and drop it into the icy waters of the Neva river.

As the frosts of December 1916 gripped St Petersburg, Rasputin sensed that his life was in danger. He became obsessed with the idea of death. As if to confirm his fears, there were loud diatribes against him in the – finally convened – Duma. Snatches of blood-curdling rumour reached him, for the loose-tongued Purishkevich had been unable to resist telling friends that a bloody fate was about to befall Rasputin. The monk began to avoid going out by day, and became suspicious of his acquaintances.

But not the pleasing Prince Yusupov. Since the plot hinged on Yusupov's ability to lure the monk to his palace, the Prince increased his friendly overtures to Rasputin. 'My intimacy with Rasputin – so indispensable to our plan – increased every day,' he wrote in his memoirs. Not only did Yusupov play the guitar for the monk but even allowed himself, claiming chest pains, to be treated with the 'miraculous magnetic strokings'. (He recorded that the power of Rasputin at such moments was almost impossible to resist.) Towards the middle of December, Yusupov invited Rasputin to spend an evening with him at his home on the Moika. Rasputin accepted.

It was around this time that Rasputin, although still not seeing where the danger to his life lay, penned his famously prophetic letter to Nicholas II. Titled 'The Spirit of Gregory Efimovich Rasputin of the village of Pokrovskoe', it read: 'I write and leave behind me this letter at St Petersburg. I feel that I shall leave my life before 1st January. I wish to make it known to the Russian people . . . If I am killed by common assassins, and especially by my brothers the Russian peasants, you, Tsar of Russia, have nothing to fear, remain on your throne and govern, and you, Russian Tsar, will have nothing to fear for your children, they will reign for hundreds of years in Russia. But if I am murdered by *boyars*, nobles, and if they shed my blood, their hands will remain soiled with my blood . . . They will leave Russia . . . if it was your relations who have wrought my death then no one of your family, that is to say, none of your children or relations will remain alive for more than two years. They will be killed by the Russian people . . . Gregory.'

The day decided on for the murder of Rasputin was 16 December. To ensure that he would be enticed to the Yusupov palace the Prince juiced the bait. He gave Rasputin to believe that Princess Irina, whose legendary beauty the monk had heard much of but never seen, would be present.

The bait was so attractive that Rasputin hardly stopped to wonder at the lateness of the hour – twelve midnight – that Yusupov wanted his presence. Others were more cautious. When Anna Vyrubova heard about the appointment she tried to dissuade Rasputin from going. Rasputin brushed away her worry.

It took all day for the conspirators to prepare the room, and it was not until late evening that they finished. Yusupov recalled the scene: 'A low, vaulted ceiling . . . walls of grey stone . . . carved chairs of wooden oak . . . A large Persian carpet covered the floor . . . In the middle of the room stood the table at which Rasputin was to drink his last cup of tea . . . On the table the Samovar smoked, surrounded by plates filled with the cakes and dainties that Rasputin liked so much . . .'

The cakes were poisoned. Dr Lazovert had injected each one with enough potassium cyanide, he calculated, to kill a dozen men.

Just before midnight, Yusupov collected the monk from his apartment and brought him to the Yusupov palace. Taking Rasputin into the cellar, the Prince promised that his wife, upstairs at party, would be down soon. Irina, in fact, was in the Crimea; the sounds of the 'party' were made by the other conspirators

Prince Felix Yusupov and his wife

and a gramophone recording of 'Yankee Doodle'.

In the cellar, Yusupov nervously handed the cakes to Rasputin. To the Prince's disbelief, Rasputin refused them. Then he changed his mind, and ate two. They had no effect. So Yusupov plied him with madeira, also poisoned. Still the monk did not writhe in agony and die. Instead, he sipped some tea to clear his head. Finishing this, he asked Yusupov, now giddy with nervous tension, to play the guitar for him. The terrified prince played one song after another, while Rasputin happily beamed on. At the top of the stairs, the other conspirators waited in a huddle, not daring to breathe.

After two hours of guitar playing, Yusupov could stand no more. He rushed upstairs to ask the others what he should do. Lazovert had fainted, Grand Duke Dimitri wanted to go home, Purishkevich suggested shooting the monk, and this opinion prevailed. Armed with a Browning revolver, Yusupov went back into the cellar. Rasputin suggested that they made a visit to the gypsy entertainers. Instead, Yusupov led the monk to a mirrored cabinet and asked him to look at the ornate silver and crystal crucifix atop it. Rasputin stared at the cross and declared that he thought the cabinet nicer. Yusupov bid him look at the crucifix again. As he did so, Yusupov shot him in the back. Rasputin fell to the floor with a scream.

On hearing the shot, Yusupov's fellow conspirators rushed downstairs. The revived Dr Lazovert pronounced Rasputin dead. His diagnosis was poor. A few minutes later, when Yusupov was alone with the body, its face twitched. 'I then saw both eyes – the green eyes of a viper – staring at me with an expression of diabolical hatred,' Yusupov remembered. Rasputin then allegedly leaped to his feet and grabbed his murderer around the neck. Yusupov broke free and scrambled up the stairs, Rasputin behind him on all fours, foaming at the mouth.

At the top of the stairs, the screaming Yusupov collided with Purishkevich, pushed him out of the way and fled into his parents' apartment. Turning, the amazed Purishkevich saw Rasputin disappear out through the front door. 'What I saw would have been a dream if it hadn't been a terrible reality. Rasputin, who half an hour before lay dying in the cellar, was running quickly across the snow-covered courtyard towards the iron gate which led to the street . . . I couldn't believe my eyes . . . But a harsh cry which broke the silence of the night persuaded me. 'Felix! Felix! I will tell everything to the Empress!' It was him all right, Rasputin. In a few seconds he would reach the iron gate.' Purishkevich took aim with his revolver. He missed twice, but his third shot hit Rasputin in the back and brought him down. A fourth shot penetrated his skull. Running to the body, Purishkevich kicked Rasputin in the temple with all of his might.

Yusupov then hit the corpse with a frenzy of blows from a club. When Rasputin no longer moved, and the snow about him had turned red, the body was bundled in a blue curtain and driven to the Neva. There, Purishkevich and Lazovert pushed it through a hole in the ice into the river.

Rasputin's body was found three days later. His lungs were full of water: he had died by drowning even though he had been poisoned, shot, and dealt mortal blows. Amazingly, he had found the strength to free one of his hands before his final moment.

The murderers of Gregory Efimovich were not hard to discover. Overcome with exultation at his shooting of the monk, Purishkevich had rushed up to a policeman and breathlessly informed him, 'I have killed Grisha Rasputin, the enemy of Russia and the Tsar.'

Regretting this impetuosity, Purishkevich later denied any part in the crime. So did the other conspirators. But the official investigation ordered by Nicholas II soon found plenty of proof of their guilt. Their immunity through Grand Duke Dmitri, however, saved them from serious punishment. Yusupov was exiled to one of his estates in the centre of Russia. Purishkevich only received a written reprimand from the palace. The Duke himself was sent to serve in Persia.

When the news of Rasputin's death became public, there was wide rejoicing. The assassins were elevated to the status of heroes. People queued to light candles beneath the icons in churches and cathedrals.

Not everybody was joyous. Predictably, the Empress was distraught at the loss of 'Our Friend'. Nicholas, too, was shaken, but his main emotion was regret that members of the Imperial family had stooped as low as murder. The disciples were inconsolable. Outside the cities, there was widespread mourning. All

The River Neva, St Petersburg

that the peasants knew of Rasputin was that he was one of them and had gone to court to tell the Tsar the truth about their lives.

Superstitious people thought his death an ill omen, and quoted a line from his letter to the Tsar: 'If I die, the Emperor will soon lose his crown . . .'

Rasputin's prophecy came to pass in slightly less than the two years he allotted. In October 1917, the workers of Russia under the leadership of the Bolshevik Party, swept away the old order into the graveyard of history. The Romanovs were executed at Ekaterinburg on 16 July 1918.

Rasputin himself was buried in secret, in a corner of the Imperial Park at Tsarskoe Selo on the bright blue morning of 3 January

1917. The Imperial family was in attendance, and hundreds of flowers were scattered on the monk's coffin. Inside, the Empress had placed two final gifts: an icon and a letter. The letter read: 'My dear martyr, give me thy blessing that it may follow me always on the sad and dreary path I have yet to follow here below. And remember us from on high in your holy prayers. Alexandra.'

FURTHER MINI SERIES INCLUDE

ILLUSTRATED POETS

Robert Burns
Shakespeare
Oscar Wilde
Emily Dickinson
Christina Rossetti
Shakespeare's Love Sonnets

FURTHER MINI SERIES INCLUDE

HEROES OF THE WILD WEST

General Custer
Butch Cassidy and the Sundance Kid
Billy the Kid
Annie Oakley
Buffalo Bill
Geronimo
Wyatt Earp
Doc Holliday
Sitting Bull
Jesse James